ON PORTSMOUTH S I.

Robert Hull

BEAFRED

First published in MMVIII by BEAFRED.

Printed in England

ISBN 978-0-9559279-0-4

CONTENTS

Arun

Maybe this is a painter's
winter morning –

impressionist
mist,

the river's
nearly Venetian
banner of glimmer,

a revelation
of small white bridge.

Then maybe a painter
would say it's a poet's morning –

that low sun
rhyming to the horizon
off pools and ditches,

alliterations
of lit post,

the off-beat rhythm
of a wavering fence.

Then again, maybe I'd say
that here and now
the woodpecker I hear
laughing off into the woods,
the waiting quiet under the trees,
the way I see empty birches lean
intently over the path

means it's my morning.

Axe

You wouldn't have left it out
inviting comparisons,

though gathering dew
overnight

probably suited it
better than yesterday's

ill-timed fit
of being wielded

on jarring heart-wood
and let skid

vertiginously
off missed edges.

Now I can't wrestle it
out of an obstinate

refusal to resume,
it won't (head hunched

in the block's
grip) relinquish

its tenacious
inertia.

From a distance
it has the posture

of The Thinker –
wondering what

it might next be hurled at,
grimly nostalgic

for the better-
aimed sort of life

it once had
with you, father.

My car

looks marooned
this morning under
the reddening sycamore –
fronds of frost
woven over it,
a scatter of leaves fallen,
paw-marks skidding
up the driver's window.

Like a modish exhibit
at a car-show.

But I'm glad a cat's
made tracks over it,
pausing to wash
in the sun I'd guess
before skidding down
the convenient windscreen
to some coin of vantage
in the sun-filled hedge.

I'm glad of the frost
and fallen leaves;
even the rust
looks right, reminder
of the decay motor
and man are heir to,
and of fools that break in.

The day's restlessness
will find me,
the bright leaves ripple off
and tear away in the rear
window whirlingly,
frost and paw-marks be effaced
by the rain that's forecast;

but when the morning's visitation
by cat and leaf and frost
is gone,
the minutes of it
will persist –

with the rust.

Beaulieu River in winter

The Earl Grey was not
available in pots
unfortunately –
or was it just not on
in pots for one? –
I forget.

Equally foregone,
the English tourist
car-park ticket, a fiver,
with free entry
to places one had no
desire to visit,
mostly moreover,
in January,
closed.

But all the river
was open, available
for miles of walking,
the light
an improbable
occasion, the air
a remission from a winter
gone to ground,
no less decommissioned,
it seemed, than the elegant old
fishing boat whose frail
wishbone of stern
lay still on the water
waiting for the tide
to turn.

And worth driving miles for,
waders' cries
searching the reaches,
a white bridge
evanescent
in hazy sun, mists
ferrying themselves
over the river.

Nearly birding

Despite reports,
the several avocets
and single spoonbill
aren't showing today
on those reedy
banks where the tide
flurries in whitely.

My binoculars only
just make out
a dead white egret
taking several seconds
to become a tattered
plastic bag,
and some serious chap
who's set up shop
on the path ahead
with tripod, thermos,
wife and telescope –
ready to identify me
as a common species
of unscholarly
stroller by water
and dilettante
wader-fancier.

He's right – you need
to be equipped
and focussed for this
birding thing;
ready to scour every inch
of near and far-away air
for a fleeting fix
of today's rare warbler.

My addiction's
more the commonplace:
the mundane
solitudes of the heron –
improbable sleuth
and hunched shaman –
and the way the 'two a penny
now' white egret in a still
reach goes dabbing
at the water and retiring
like a brisk painter at a canvas.

And today in winter twilight
my trip is towards the place
where redshank flute
insistent protest
at each step I take
and a whole field of curlew
calling rise as one.

Gull

The beach
is a new place each morning

the gull
cries it into being cries

the sun on the water
the ships in the offing

cries new
wrecks of wrack
new continents
of pebble

cries Hamish in his pool
barking
to his owners calling
'Hamish! Hamish!'

cries light
on wet flint

and prints
of naked feet
and cycle wheels
and perfect whorls
of some thing
receding inwards
as the beach inhales

cries wind
driving sand
to founder
over inch-high
precipices of meander

cries Hamish still
won't let go his pool

The beach
is a new place
each morning

the gull
cries it into being.

'Tres faciunt collegium' at the Dell

Three of them, in their thirties
in front of us all season
on their feet fist-shaking
at f'ing skeg welsh black eytie wop frog
brazilian northern and assorted
other bastards.

Behind them every game
we moan at blind refs
and the berks running the line,
behind them amongst schoolkids
wince at their jaunty hatreds.

Half time –
West Ham at home –
two of them groom each other,
feeling out No 2 cuts,
scrutinising ears
for flaky bits.

Then cupped choric hands again
baying retribution –
You Judas Berkovitz!

By Monday they'll have forgotten,
back in the Transit
punching each other full of ladness,
thrashing down the M 27 in the wet.

We tap a shoulder now and then:

Excuse me, would you mind not....?

S'what we come for mate.

But

they just might stop
if we keep at it – the way
if we keep playing like this
we should avoid the drop,

could even come top
some sunny day – the day
one of their mums
comes

to take them home.

Bashoing on regardless –
after hearing 16 translations of the famous poem by Basho:

Furu–ike / ya / kawazu / tobi–komu / mizu–no–oto
Old pond / : / frog / jump–in / water–sound

Lots of ways
say famous frog-poem
by old Basho:

Like: 'Old Japan
jump-in-pond
frog-sound!'

'Ancient plop!
Pond jumped in
by frog!'

'Old frog echo
pond plop-in
sound.'

'Frog-plop –
sound of old pond
being jumped in.'

Lots of ways,
all ok – so long as
in Japan-ese!

Too many non–Japan
poet go on about
old frog plop-in.

Suggest non-Japan
poet try own plop-in
story-line, like:

'Splash! student
nod off listening too
many old haiku.'

'Splash! please student
can have old temple
ball back?'

'Splash! Basho
chuck more translator
in old pond! Yaa!'

'No splash. Old pond
empty, closed for cleaning.
Sad poet hop off.'

Bosho [1935–   ]

Brief report

It gleams like the sun on the river mud,
the barrel of the gun
he's just carried past me
under the flowering summits of early May.

I imagine it won't be turned on the thrush
I've just been listening to,
sounding from the top of an ash
in cockaded leaf, half-green at last,
or the swan reconnoitring
the stillness of the silted-up
old tidal meander.

I'd sooner not wonder what creature,
trying out earth's grass
or venturing over its air,
civilised man at leisure
will fix his sights on.

I'd sooner not wait –

on this fervent
hymn of an evening,
while the rabbits are out and about
in frisking convention
and I hear from the river
the mallard's dashing aquatics
and branchers rasp and caw
in the rookery's gloaming –

for the sound of it.

May 5th

As advertised, a Festival
of Flowers in the cathedral,
legions of cut
blooms leant, laid out,
tenderly arrested, envased.

Within the portals of The Word,
beneath sunlit clerestories,
the flower of the world,
to be worshipped, regarded, filed past –
the cost of it, modest.

Out in the world, under the downs,
a place apart – the ash in first leaf,
martins come again
to describe how the sky
arcs over a field where days-old
calves tilt and teeter,
and on the Arun's choked meander
round by Burpham, a few
swallows to be grateful for.

Choirs of kingcups
at its tide-arrested edge,
in the reeds the manic liturgy
of the invisible sedge warbler,
a swan slowly, sacramentally
wrestling out a spear of green
to sail nestwards with it.

Fences, outbuildings, footpath signs
clouding white, as blossom
yields daily to blossom.

And it costs me nothing,
my ticket to wander
amongst the day's
condemned splendour.

Lit poplars finally,
almost post-festivally
as evening comes in,
over towards Bury.

Amen
to this and these and those
and them.

Countrysiding

Stumbling over roots
on Stane Street,
the Solent gleaming
west, Worthing
the other way,
Butlins at Bognor
white-tilt-tented
as if fabled
just down there
in my binoculars,
taking pictures
of lambs frisking
no-one's pockets
and clouds sprawled
at rest on Bignor,
stalking every
gatekeeper
that floats my way,
at ease under
the ash in flower,
the lark ascending.

All this passive
consumption of quiet
and stillness and
nothing-happening-
ness when I could be
actively countrysiding –
fishing, riding,
playing pub cricket,
supporting a fete,
harrassing something,
urging my Isuzu Trooper
down the outback trails
behind Chichester.

Except that I'm
fine thanks up here,
practising anonymity,
feeling affinity
with solitary
and social bee,
with binoculars
to help me steer clear
of geared-up bikers
and caparisoned walkers
in groups with maps
in plastic folders;

ready to receive
this brightest of wheatears
coming momentarily
to grace the grass,
the speckled wood
trying out the path
every few yards
in front of me
in the sun.

Littlehampton today

is almost
Mediterranean –

the shimmering
sea's sheer opal
where a fishing boat
planes up
its scarf of silver

the haze of dunes
rising from the glitter
that might be a far dim spur
of the Taigetus.

No matter
that where the taverna
serving Amstel and kalamari
at 11 am should be
stand stolid beach-huts
municipally minded;

no matter
it's all too English

from traditional
pitch and putt
and whimsically jolly
little diesel steam train
with miniature whoop

to melancholy
excesses of flesh
tattoo-burdened
and overly sunned
feeding fish and chips
to harbour swans –

no matter for once all that –

I'll celebrate
with the little train today
with a miniature whoop
for a Littlehampton
gone almost Mediterranean.

Storm

A ship offloaded it all
near Selsey in a storm
someone said,
so the wood's scattered
along the beaches
like exploded fencing,
or remnants of piano
from a Marx Brothers film.

And now it's a calm sunny morning
and a man with his dog
is proceeding
with a plank under each arm
along the prom.
A white van parked up
bristles like a missile silo.
And two ladies are on their way
through the rose gardens
sharing the burden
of five foot of pine
that looks just right.

In an hour or so the tide's swell
might well
heave in more
shattered pallets, more timber
in unusable sizes, more would-be
shelving for greenhouse
or conservatory,
more wreck and trophy
to make off with pretending
we've something in mind.

Reserve, early morning

At first
the water's a plinth of ebony.

Then light begins.

Soon there are curlew homing in
from the dark's turning.

The oyster-catcher
makes an impassioned plea
for dawn to be held a while longer
in its newness.

Then shadow pulling back.

The white of egrets
poking around like tourists
looking for breakfast, uncertain,

dunlin trickling like grain
down the mud-banks,

redshank flittering, probing.

Shimmers of sound, voices, callings.

It's like a rehearsal, or tuning up,
the gentle whole wide quiet noise of it.

The light rises, and rises.

River

The Rother
doesn't advertize

its hidden bridges,
its undisturbed

haunts for picnics
under shimmering

willows. Its magical
places lie beyond

the summons
of footpath signs.

Over sagging stiles
you walk to them

past old barns,
by reedy streams

and ways not known
to just anyone,

where tall grasses
already dry

in beautiful early
June lean awry.

Scrapyard

Here are tiles
come down from roofs
beds that walked
bricks returned
from buildings disbanded.

Here are railings guarding
railings ladders climbing
ladders chimneys that stopped
smoking doors
that have forgotten
the art of concealment.

Here alongside outdoor furniture
with no future
baths recline
in a state
amongst rain-filled sinks
that list in weedy torpor
header tanks
brought to earth and ensuites
no longer discreet.

Here dispirited statuary
finds sanctuary –
a clinically demure
Venus under a blue wire
pergola, a bouncer-
gladiator propositioning
a pastoral personage
draped in vinery.

But here also old sideboards
rise transfgured
from baths of acid,
here saw-blades
shine again and things
of bronze with wings.

And here lay scattered
the bricks I took to fashion
a fish in my garden;
here waited
the care-worn cupboard
that summons to its grainy door
the sun each mid mid-winter
at 3 pm in our kitchen.

And here's the curator
and sanctuary priest
who brings by aside and anecdote
illumination to each transaction
and object lesson, today's
being the seven species of lichen
on these staddle-stones
he half-hopes won't sell.

Here's to him too because
in the midst of commerce
we are in life for once,
because as I kneel
to ask if the rear wheel
of this prone old bicycle
that clicks like a death-watch beetle
will rise and spin freely again
and he says it will

I believe.

Gnome's Tale

Now I lie face down
with an arm gone.

I was fifth from left
in the second row.

I watched her enter,
consider the wrapped herons

a moment, and walk outside.
The drowsing white

carp would please her,
or the terracotta containers

for lobelias.
But neither those

nor any coloured
singing bird

was what she wanted.
Instead she paused

in front of us,
and before every

accomplished pixy,
fey wheelbarrow

and ever-grazing duck,
chose me.

She gave me a lake
to gaze across,

and woodland to guard.
She made me keeper

of all the fish
that lift to the light

and drift downards.
She appointed me

official listener
to all the grass.

I had a position
near her words,

and heard her pleasure
in the darkeness

as her movement woke
the scent of flowers.

I intended her to know
my loyalty,

my steadfast gratitude
for all this.

I would not flinch
from weather.

She would see how year
in year out

I would not tilt an inch
from true.

Dancing with the Arun

I only leaned on my stick a bit to prod
a beech log floating in the reeds and push it
towards midstream. The log must have rolled

and the stick slipped under it because the river
was up round me in no time with its abrupt welcome.
As I held my arms out over it like a cormorant drying

or someone slowly wading a darkened room
the afternoon turned suddenly breathlessly cold
as the river urged me firmly along the bank

with the sort of quietly insistent pressure I remember
a tall brown-suited grey-haired male dancing teacher
propelled me along with once and once only

at Worsley's Dance Hall's morning learners' class.
Elbows came in handy – without them I couldn't
have fetched up even at third attempt with a newt-like

squirming heave onto the bank, stretched full length
and floundering like some washed-up old amphibian
or species of odd clothed fish unknown to science.

Newly preserved from drowning I went squelching
past June afternoon walkers looking puzzled
at the sight of so much darkly stained clothing,

and wondering what the sound of my boots meant,
and I even began to congratulate myself
on strolling freely down a sunny lane soaking

past families with dogs and staring kids to the car,
imagining how I'd explain at home, with something
like a reckless grin, how 'I fell in'. Then,

as I sank into the front seat, dragging off boots
and dark socks, a small brown reminder of river
came meandering from under the accelerator,

and I felt myself taken by the shoulder again,
feet tangling with each other a bit awkwardly,
being urged along the Arun's lonely dance-floor.

Fortissimo

By the open front door
the last bars of some Bruckner

detain me in the car
under accompanying thunder.

Loud light jigs down, shattering
all heaven round me.

I hurry in,
put some lights on.

In the quiet of the kitchen,
only the last of the rain

diminuendo

through a window left open

on the fig-leaves' tympani

pianissimi.

Sunset on the prom

No-one turns to look

Not the cyclist
in sheer gear
shiny black hat
sun-glasses
or dawdlers
waiting for dogs to pee
or the girl
yearning into her mobile

Only two old sorts a-stroll
observe as he pauses
at a drinking fountain
'e's lost 'alf 'is bike

Meanwhile

as the jet-skier
fifty yards out
bouncing along
fast and furiously
on his crotch
falls off again

and the last light
heads away
into the sunset

the mono-cyclist
most driven
of stylitics
no stylist
pedals
his self-
inflicted
single-
wheel mill
furiously
but not fast
towards the full
moon rising
not furiously
but fast
over Butlins
in the east.

Sibelius 2

It never seems quite right these days –
the slow movement languid
or the fast driven,
not enough coarse vibrancy
in the brass,
the horns less than haunting.

An elderly thing maybe,
going back,
finding so much music's
so much brilliance
not wholly felt.

Fifty-five years ago,
a summer evening,
the Halle
under John Barbirolli
at Preston Public Hall –
his hands
shaping the air to sound
I haven't heard since.

The passion
epic in that face
travelled with me in the dark
of the carriage window
on the last train home.

Sometimes memory
leans on the long brass rail
looking down
to where Sibelius climbed
from whispered intimations
of lakeside and forest
to summits of thunder,

and hears again
in an after-shock of silence,
the sumptuous pianissimo
of granite falling open.

The Youth Hostel

was a long time ago –
train to Glasgow,
a lift on the back of a lorry
along Loch Lomond,
a hike from the station
over Rannoch Moor.

A bucket on an arcing rope
hurled out over the loch
from the landing stage
and hauled in dripping
those chill mornings
was our water.

The rest's gone –
except for deer
on the fading horizon,
an eagle circling,
the two of us quarreling.

Five hundred miles
for a few days' wilderness
and some callow acrimony –

but the bucket arcing out
over the loch
still breaks in glitter
the sleeping dark water,
is still hauled in
dripping with first light
fifty years later.

Summer 2005

Trying to find where the Solent Way
goes next, I see the M27
is due to open in late 1974.

Hardly surprising –
prescience not being
a map's thing –
you had no inkling
of the existence of a Millenium
prom complete with marina
and fibre-glass armada.

All those years of advising me
what rivers, hills and pubs
to aspire to,
all the time letting me slip
further and further
behind the times…

It seems I need a guide
more informed,
tattered companion,
if I'm to stay abreast
of events, in touch –

though having to desert you for another
doesn't mean we can't savour together
a few more resplendent minutes
of not knowing quite where we are.

Boots

Hail and snowfall
kept them supple,
springy moss,
stones over becks,
handfuls of dubbin
ritually laid on.

Now they're cracked
as any fell-face,
ravaged as a tarn
in a March wind.

Stout pilgrims
who led me to safety
more than once,
they've hurried down
off white tops
in frosty twilights
threatening snow,
stepped out refreshed
to make the best
of sunlit mornings
wet with dew.

Now they won't venture
a foot further
along sharp ridges
in swirling mist –
or slog on any more
in mid-summer
up aching paths
by glittering becks –
or put a spurt on
along a lakeshore
under lowering thunder.

They're down finally
from summit, cloud
and col to take up
modest lodging
on this window-ledge,
beyond the last
thundering force
and vertiginous edge.

Simmy

Old cat on my lap,
I thought you'd go first,
not your lovelier twin sister,
that charmer incapable
of inelegance of gesture
who could turn spitfire
nevertheless, little
though she was.
And now there's her grave
under the ash.
A month later,
I no longer watch out –
though I think you still do –
from this favourite chair
of mine she made hers
once the upholsterers
renewed its faded appeal;
I no longer wait for her
to come trotting
up the garden again,
bright-eyed as ever,
furry saddle-bags
of slack tum swinging,
to sniff you a welcome
and proffer me a quick
'ach' of greeting.
Do you remember
how she'd disappear for hours,
and I'd ask you,
Where's your sister?
Old cat on my lap,
we have our answer.

Encounter with hard hat

Stepping on site at this Major
Sewage Works by a temporary
Cheltenham road closure
I reflect I've survived

walks with you without
this sort of hat.
Installed uncertainly
in a portakabin I survey
your littered desk, with the day's

firmly scrawled action
list, and a projection –
a hardly surprising
steadily rising

curve – of Cheltenham's future
sewage needs.
It finally persuades
me, daughter,
that the forceful hurrying

handwriting known for so long
is performing tunneling
and major road closure
on Cheltenham.

High tide

Seaside autumn.
The dodgems are in hibernation.
All the rides are ridden.

There are only a few loiterers
staring from under umbrellas
at the sand that's still summer yellow,
the hard rain pimpling the harbour,
the tide turning back the river
that's rising and rising
in the harbour in the rain.

The low sky deepens
to dark on each horizon.
Lights are on.

Surely the tide's high enough,
surely it's finished coming in –
when men from the last fishing–boat
churning past in the rain
can peer into the tea-shops
on the harbour-road
and read the menus outside.

One day sometime,
on an afternoon like this,
the tide will keep rising
and rising and some of the land
will come to an end.

The corner-pub will need stilts then.
The fairground
will be the foreshore,
only the castle with its tower
and the high rides will be open.

One day sometime,
one of the casual loiterers
bemused by the rising waters
will be caught unawares
and have to scramble the crinkly slide
to the crenellated battlements
and ask one of the stiffly gleaming
chocolate box soldiers
guarding the security light
if he could shelter inside
till the next – if there is one –
ebb tide.

On Portsmouth station,

a policeman
with a gun on his arm

arresting my
leisurely progress.

It flashes into mind
that if I look directly

down the barrel
of his vision

I might awaken the glint
of intent scrutiny,

and this sixty-something,
uncertain-looking

Caucasian male
with a faded rucksack

and the appearance
of being somewhat

abandoned by life, maybe,
or success or a woman

or all three, might seem
to a young man

carrying state-sanctioned
rapid-action hardware

to have been left behind
suspiciously unattended.

Larkin (1922 – 1985)

Like cloud-shadow today,
your death making its way

across England, across its towns,
counties, fields, lanes.

Slowly over cranes and spires
and neglected waters,

along quiet branch-lines,
over college lawns

like cloud-shadow it passes,
darkening recreation-grounds,

estates with washing
and slow widening

rivers. And you, going
ahead, at summer's pace cycling

down one of the lost lanes
at the end of the fens,

listening already
to oblivion whispering

from dusty stillnesses
where flowering grasses

hide the place-names.
In one of those faded Junes

you found somewhere
the start of a war –

queues of men, grinning
as if they were on the winning

team already,
the innocently

lived years ending
in spendthift gesture.

Few such poems, all too few,
but no-one reproaches you

with this last silence,
though perhaps it means

you've let the literateurs
loose round canals and choirs

to finally hunt you down.
But you'll be left decently alone

by the less well-read
your compassion celebrated –

those being pushed to the side
of their own lives,

or adrift between garish wedding
and drab bed-sitter.

They'd be the best people
to come forward –

though they might never have heard
of you, it's they who could

best speak in your memory
their own felt testimony,

like an awkward 'Here endeth'
pronounced quite loudly enough.

'Fine lawn seed'

The box is limp,
the seed inside gone
soft and dry and grey,
its prophecy
of fine lawn
sifted to disillusion.

And now the sun's
sudden revelation
spills in,
and small moths
it's been months
of nourishment for
twirl upwards
in alarmed hundreds
dusting my face.

They spin
greyly away
from their dusty
seminary,
carrying over
lawn and roses
myriad fresh hopes
for the downfall
of pear, quince, apple.

Letter

In my copy of Elizabeth Bishop's
Complete Poems –
1970, the earlier one –
is folded a letter of hers
that's not in *Elizabeth Bishop's Letters*.
Friends of mine met her
on a boat to somewhere –
Brazil I think – in the sixties;
and somehow it transpired
as they say in fiction
that she wrote
this graceful helpful note
to an anonymous nobody
about his not all that
crafted scribblings.
I never thought
of trying to write back.
When the flimsy page
came in two, I sellotaped
it back in one
and sort of mounted it.
It's on Blue Star
note-paper, typed,
with a few words underlined.
I've kept it all these years,
hoping she wouldn't mind
that knowledge of a particular
generosity of hers
stayed confined
for so long to a few friends
and now this rather more
I hope – thanks to her –
crafted verse.

Private river

'You can't go this way mate
it's private.'
I can't go near it
where it glints in October sun

winding south
between nice new barbed wire fences
glinting in the sun
as they wind south.

Private
the red paint says
fresh as red roses
Private Private,

while the fence-posts glisten
with new
private dew.
Meanwhile shadows of clouds

who obviously can't read
go clambering over the fences
not taking any notice
of any notice

or of the herons
standing there
maintaining surveillance;
while the clouds' reflections

swim lazily across the river
taking all the time in the world.
Not one is arrested,
though heaven knows what damage

lots of heavy dark clouds
or their reflections might do
just wandering about
where it's private.

As for my dog and I
who like to wander like a cloud
and watch the day go by,
we can see from here – we're not allowed

to see from there – how peaceful
a private river is,
how private a peaceful river is
when it flows gently,

when it gleams invitingly
between nice new fences,
running quietly
the right way through England.

The Graveyard by Croston Church School

Bury me here
by Yarrow River,
near the wooden bridge
the children skip over;
bury me here
where the river goes under.

Bury me here
where their voices shriek
across the churchyard
five a days a week;
bury me here
near schoolroom clamour.

Bury me here
where waiting mums
gossip and peer
in each other's prams;
bury me here
where I'm part of a future.

Bury me here
where the paving-stones
on this glistening path
are old gravestones;
bury me here
for the rain to walk over.

Bury me here
where flowers are tended,
where little is said
and no grief mended;
bury me here
where the love-lorn linger.

Bury me here
under the bells
that fall to quiet
as the church fills:
Bury me here
when the ringing's over.

Bury me here
where I was born,
near silent orchards
and ripening corn.
Bury me here
in a quiet corner.

Hands

Folded
and finished
seven years ago.

I remember them
in football crowds,
crossing roads.

I see them
driving your old Rover,
in the next room

writing, reaching
to welcome me home. Seven
years ago today

they held a racket,
cut flowers,
wrote me a letter,

and carrying a tray up
late at night
clutched at the stairs.

The Lakes

Waking in youth hostels
to the beck's soft speech.

Far companionable days
on the tops in winter,
the high falls frozen over,
icicled red in the greying sun.

Three of us
rowing round Derwentwater
one morning in September,
tying up at a narrow jetty
to call at the public bar
of the old Borrowdale Arms –
the Lodore Falls now,
long gone to top-notch kitsch
and jetting tourist.

Snowed-under Ambleside,
New Year's Eve at the YWCA
amongst Swedish girls.

Long trips up
from Sussex for half-terms
at the farm in Watendlath,
our children's voices
clamorous over beck and tarn.

Snatched couples of days
in late autumn, Coniston
misty-still, blue-skyed, edged
with bronze bracken.

A week at Tilberthwaite
in April, fells under snow,
slushy paths sunlit –
pictures of you
picnicking by a beck,
climbing a slope towards me
somewhere near Elterwater,
looking happy.

Almost a life-time
of images that fade faster
as they get nearer.

Speckled wood

It settled on my page
a minute ago –

yellow-speckled
brown-black wings
illuminating
for a moment
the sunlit margin
of the afternoon –

then looped across
to the lip of my glass,
rose to greet
an apple leaf and made
its flickering way
down a grove
of wilting loose-strife –
and was gone.

The book of verse
open on my lap
flexes in a stir
of south-west air
restrained
earth-bound wings.

Threat

For the sake of security
I am negotiating carefully
a muddy path by the river,

leading to a bridge which
for the sake of security
the wind has cleared of fallen leaves.

Beneath me the tide
backs up slowly
so as not to alarm anybody,

while a pale sun
moves with self-effacing vigilance
behind clouds.

A cautious morning
that is in danger nonetheless
of negligently
slipping towards spring –

its lapses of attention
evident in the unguarded laughter
of the woodpecker
looping into woods
beyond the sun's
fitful surveillance,

the careless demeanour
of these snowdrops
under the probing scrutiny
of merciless air.

But I'm uneasily aware
that in the intent stillness
to left and right
of this strangely songless
woodland ride
lurks the renewed threat
of light snow.

Walking with J

In step
at times but
mainly not.

You fall back
at any lamb
with a limp

or small bird
insisting
on being heard

through.
Frail moths
detain you,

smart arm-
waving insects
string you along.

We're late
you say
dropping out

to listen
to more lichen
or examine

a paring
of air,
then hurry

to study
at a tarn
rich in

irrestistible
tadpole
and bog-bean.

Our sandwiches
unfinished,
friends

wait on time
somewhere. I'm
ready, you're

rifling unlikely
grasses. I
stride;

your
pace is
curious.

Super 8

I watch it through again,
looking towards you up
the steep white stream-slope
where thirty-odd years ago
you splash up lumps
of wet light in the sun's eye.

They're more believable
in the memory, the path
up from Watendlath,
the bracken you wade through –
hair less aflame than film insists –
lit with October hues
no camera could remember.

And Langstrath didn't glint
in such soft focus,
or that chain of geese
trail overhead in quite
so intense a blueness.

This half-term morning
you might well be looking up
a steep white ski-slope
somewhere near Moutiers,
taking moving pictures
of your children splashing
and shouting in snow.

Maybe you'll do it better;
maybe you'll not later –
watching round again
the distant cavorting
of your young charges –
wonder if looking back
might not be easier
without such images.

Tide walk

A wavering yard-
and-a-half-wide path
between a scarp
of pebble and stone
and the trail of wrack
the tide deposits
as each failing
wave's flowing
contour-line
reaches in
in varying arcs
to darken the yellow
sand by my feet.
Ephemeral
and never to be
seen again as it is,
this narrow space
I walk in
images all those
transient tracks
by which one goes,
and only goes,
and which don't permit
journeys back.